Llamas as Pets

Keeping Llamas As Pets

Llama raising and breeding, where to buy, care, housing tips, cost, health, handling, diet, and much more included!

By: Lolly Brown

Copyrights and Trademarks

All rights reserved. No part of this book may be reproduced or transformed in any form or by any means, graphic, electronic, or mechanical, including photocopying, recording, taping, or by any information storage retrieval system, without the written permission of the author.

This publication is Copyright ©2019 NRB Publishing, an imprint. Nevada. All products, graphics, publications, software and services mentioned and recommended in this publication are protected by trademarks. In such instance, all trademarks & copyright belong to the respective owners. For information consult www.NRBpublishing.com

Disclaimer and Legal Notice

This product is not legal, medical, or accounting advice and should not be interpreted in that manner. You need to do your own due-diligence to determine if the content of this product is right for you. While every attempt has been made to verify the information shared in this publication, neither the author, neither publisher, nor the affiliates assume any responsibility for errors, omissions or contrary interpretation of the subject matter herein. Any perceived slights to any specific person(s) or organization(s) are purely unintentional.

We have no control over the nature, content and availability of the web sites listed in this book. The inclusion of any web site links does not necessarily imply a recommendation or endorse the views expressed within them. We take no responsibility for, and will not be liable for, the websites being temporarily unavailable or being removed from the internet.

The accuracy and completeness of information provided herein and opinions stated herein are not guaranteed or warranted to produce any particular results, and the advice and strategies, contained herein may not be suitable for every individual. Neither the author nor the publisher shall be liable for any loss incurred as a consequence of the use and application, directly or indirectly, of any information presented in this work. This publication is designed to provide information in regard to the subject matter covered.

Neither the author nor the publisher assume any responsibility for any errors or omissions, nor do they represent or warrant that the ideas, information, actions, plans, suggestions contained in this book is in all cases accurate. It is the reader's responsibility to find advice before putting anything written in this book into practice. The information in this book is not intended to serve as legal, medical, or accounting advice.

Foreword

Llamas are the classified as *camelis* from the *camelidae* family. They are animals that are generally considered livestock by many, however, most people lucky enough to get up close and personal with a llama would tell you that, given enough time for the llama to get to know you, the more you'll realize how smart and sociable these big babies are. Llamas are social animals that if properly socialized, make very calm, gentle companions. They are great additions to families who have livestock and barnyard animals. Not only are they great companions and packers on long trail walks, they are also great livestock guardians.

People, most especially, city-folk wouldn't think of keeping a llama as a pet. Not in the traditional sense, at least. First of all, most people from the city don't have enough space a llama would need to thrive, much less a couple. But the llama, with its cheerful disposition has been capturing more and more animal lovers and we are seeing a number of facilities which are fit to house and raise llamas. Llamas were introduced to the United States sometime in the early

1900 and has recently gained better visibility and chatter amongst farm owners, and pet lovers. Llamas are now frequent participants in 4H shows, fairs and petting shows because of their docile characteristic.

Often times, llama ownership comes about from a case of someone falling in love with the animal by chance. Of course, llamas are not for everyone. This become quite apparent immediately upon seeing one, given their size and needs. Llamas can only be suitably paired with those who have a deep commitment for raising animals well and who would be able to have enough room to house them. Llamas thrive best with their sort close by and should not be kept by its lonesome.

They are not small animals, weighing in at 250 to 500 lb., and being anywhere from 5' to 6"5' tall, so they will need an ample amount of space. Llamas have been given a bad rap about spitting, but this behavior is more typical between llamas and, unless poorly socialized, is usually not directed at people. Aside from the comical look of perpetual cheekiness, they also make a variety of sounds, adding to the entertainer-factor of the llama. With a lifespan estimated between the ranges of 15 to 30 years, they are likely companions for the long haul, as long as you learn how to care for and raise them properly - not to mention getting the proper sort of help they would need when and if the need arises.

Here is where we step in and get you in on the low-down on how to care for llamas. You will discover tips and methods on how to raise llamas successfully with the help of a few people you will definitely need to network with. You will find that raising llamas is much like raising kids, because you will need the support of individuals who will be vital in filling in gaps of its care that you would otherwise not be able to provide readily or with the proper expertise. Delve in and get to know this awesome beast of burden that has enthralled the hearts of many pet lovers. You will not only get to know the general traits, history and features of the llama, you will also discover what it would take to find a brood of these furry beasts and how to correctly raise and train them, allowing you and your loved ones years of fun and companionship with them.

Table of Contents

Introduction: Welcome to the World of Llamas! 1

Chapter One: All about Llamas 3

    History of Llamas 4

    Llamas at Work 7

Chapter Two: Llamas as Pets 11

    Before You Get One! 12

    Things to Remember When Keeping Llamas as Pets 13

Chapter Three: Getting Acquainted with Llamas 19

Chapter Four: Some Facts about Llamas 27

    Appearance 28

    Characteristics 29

    Behavior 32

Chapter Five: Requirements When Raising Llamas 35

    Requirements 36

    Necessities 38

Chapter Six: Health Concerns and Care 43

    Tips When Feeding and Caring For Llamas 44

    Common Illnesses 46

        Abscess 46

        Bare Nose 48

        Berserk Male Syndrome 48

    Blue Eye Syndrome 49

    Drooping Eye 49

    Digestive System 50

    Fighting Teeth 51

    Heat Stress 51

    Lice 52

    Lump on Jaw 53

    Mange 54

    Meningeal Worm 54

    Ringworm 55

    Toenails 56

    Vaccinations 57

Chapter Seven: Husbandry Practices for Llamas 59

    Haltering 61

    Keep It Short - Sessions 63

    Fits is Important 64

    It's a Matter of Trust 65

    Buckled 66

    Resistance 67

    Slow Your Hands Down 68

Chapter Eight: Barn Maintenance and Litter Boxes 71

    The Litter Box 72

    Litter Training Your Llamas 73

    Labor Saver 75

    Extra Care Saves You Plenty 77

Chapter Nine: Reasons You Should Add Llamas to Your Livestock Herd 79

    Benefits of Keeping a Llama 80

        Llamas for Protection 81

        Llama Care 83

        Housing for Llamas 85

        Guarding Against Human Predators 85

        Other Benefits 86

Chapter 10: Summary and Care Sheet 89

Photo Credits 103

References 105

Introduction: Welcome to the World of Llamas!

Llamas wouldn't, obviously, be a pet of choice one would readily jump to, most especially if you have not met one face to face. But these lovable beasts have been gaining fast popularity because of their friendly disposition and calm demeanor. For starters, llamas are big animals. Bigger than the largest dog you can think of. With their weight averaging between 250 to about 500 pounds, they certainly aren't what you would call compact. Because llamas have

Introduction: Welcome to the World of Llamas!

long been used to help people haul goods, they tend to be more comfortable interacting with us.

Unless you grew up in the high plains of the Andes in South America, you would probably never have considered llamas to be a pet much less a companion. But, families from the Andes have been working side by side with llamas for a very long time. Here we find that they are not only part of the family, but also integral factor to the income and livelihood of families living there. However, with the luxury of travel export, and improving local breeding practices, llamas has become one of the fastest growing unusual pets of today.

Families with spacious land area, and who work well with livestock, farm animals have discovered the lovable attributes of llamas and have added them to the roster of animals they raise in their farms even those who live in the city and have no provisions for space, have actually found ways to satisfy their love for raising these lovable animals that, city living has not stopped them from caring for a few of them as a herd.

Chapter One: All about Llamas

People living in South America have long before learnt and have experienced the useful trait of the llama as a packing-animal. They are generally used as aid to transport possessions on wild terrain. They are naturally agile, strong and built for the job of packing. They are also pretty calm animals who make perfect companions for a long hike on, sometimes, inhospitable terrain - making the journey easier and more easy-going. Aside from this, their feet have soft, leathery pads which help their footing. Their soft pads help by causing little damage to vegetation on the trail.

Chapter One: All About Llamas

Llamas were brought to the shores of the United States in the 1900s. This chapter will provide you facts and historical backgrounds of Llamas.

History of Llamas

The domestication of llamas and their close cousins, the alpacas, paved the way for its place in the ranks of farm animals in North America by the 1800s. This is largely owed to William Randolph Heart, a rich, influential business magnate of the 1900s who brought in a great many of these beautiful beasts of burden to populate the land he owned. Along with other farm animals that resided on the Hearst estate, was some llamas and other exotic species. To date, the Hearst llama collection of a dozen is the largest herd imported from overseas. After an incident of FMD (Foot and Mouth Disease) the importation of llamas was banned. All importation seen after 1930 came from nearby Canada with more than a few of these importations carried out illegally.

Most of these early imports were zoo residents or part of private collections until the 1970s when the early imports became the startup pool of llamas that was to grow the

Chapter One: All About Llamas

population in the U.S. Being that it was an exotic species, people did not see the need to foster an aggressive breeding program or work on managing breeding practices. Back then, hybridization and inbreeding practices were common. There were, however, a few private breeders and zoos that recognized the unique qualities of the llama. These private groups started administering more desirable management of the breeding methods resulting in more favorable results in terms of animal health.

These were the initial herds which heightened the awareness of humans on the beauty, grace and use of these animals. The presentation of the improved and better bred llamas made people take notice and many had started to see the docility of the llama. They had started to learn of the many useful things they can do side-by-side with these already, long-standing workers from the Andes, and began taking in and rearing these magnificent, friendly beasts as pack animals as well as pets and companions. As years passed, individuals who had been raising these funny-faced looking camelids began seeing the many advantageous traits of the llamas that actually pulled weight around a farm.

Chapter One: All About Llamas

By the late seventies, market momentum on the acquisition of llamas began to build. The demand for llamas became so great that the supply was not able to keep up with the clamor for the beautiful beasts. This impacted the increase of the price of the llama in the livestock and pet trade, making many of the interested individuals wait for at least a year, to two, for their llamas.

Since demand outstripped the demand, and waiting lists became a common routine with most breeders, a move was made to lift the ban on import restrictions. After decades of fighting to amend the restrictions, bans on flying in llamas were allowed once again and when llamas were given access and entered the U.S. again.

The cost of transportation and quarantines saw that limited numbers (of several thousands) came into the country. These imports after the ban, along with the original pool of bred llamas that were already in the country, currently represent the population of llamas available in the US.

Chapter One: All About Llamas

Llamas at Work

So popular has the llama become of its abilities to take on and carry heavy loads, as well as its amiable and friendly demeanor, llamas have been the long, constant companions of residents of the high puna of the Andes that finding them on golf greens has become more and more of a norm. Llamas are great companions during camping and hiking trips. They are such great companions along trails and such strong packers who can carry up to 50-65 pounds. Packing llamas are able to help along older backpackers and nature hikers to continuing what they love. They all have different personalities like people. Some are quiet, and others are just a little quirkier. Treat it with respect and they will give you back the same.

Farm raised llamas have been trained to cart, which can be more of a challenge without the proper sort of equipment, however totally possible with the right implements. Because llamas are clever beasts able to repeat actions with proper training and socialization along with the properly built-to-fit cart, they will be able to carry out this task. They are calm animals who are wonderful companion packers on mountain treks and hikes. They allow people to

Chapter One: All About Llamas

enjoy the hike without having to lug around all that poundage that goes along with camping.

Don't be too surprised to find a matter of llamas on golf greens, caddying golf bags of clubs because of their penchant for cleanliness, their easy trainability and readiness to be around humans make them suitable candidates. And with soft, leathery pads for feet, they step lightly causing almost no harm to the tended greens of golf courses that choose to employ these friendly beasts.

The fur produced by the llama has long been used to create rugs and yarn. The strong consistency of the fiber as well as fineness of it depends largely on the area of the llama the fur was taken. Aside from these already many positive traits of the llama, it has also been noted that llamas and children, with the proper socialization and training (for both animal and child) get along really well.

This is why llamas have found its way into the ranks of other farm animals at 4H projects, parades and pet shows, fast becoming a favorite amongst many young humans. With proper socialization and given the proper circumstances for training, llamas can become a candidate to

Chapter One: All About Llamas

work in animal-assisted therapy. Due to their friendly demeanor, many llamas are now certified therapy animals, helping in the recuperation and coping techniques to those who require their help.

Llamas raised in farms have been found to have a natural penchant to be protective of other farm animals. as an extension of their nature, they are given posts as sentry to other livestock who inhabit farms. They are able to give alert and raise awareness of predator lurking in the area which may cause harm and damage to livestock of the farm. They may not be the best in giving physical protection to ward off animal attacks, but they are definitely alert and talented in getting the attention of their owners.

They have simple dietary needs that are economical and will not take up too much of your llama-funds. Being the herbivores they are, llamas mainly prefer hay or grass to munch on. Llamas are big animals weighing in at 20 to 30 lbs. at birth. They are hardy animals who live up to thirty years. The gestation period for a pregnant llama is approximated at 11 ½ months. Make sure that you are aware of what to look out for in cases of pregnancy. Breeding

Chapter One: All About Llamas

llamas can be something that you will purposely aim for or a happy accident, being owner of a few llamas.

The coarser fiber llamas produce may not be as in-demand like the finer alpaca fur, but there is a growing market for the use of llama fur. Homesteaders and artisans have found a number of uses of the thicker fiber that llamas produce and use them for wall hangings, rugs, carpets.

Llama fleece come in a multitude of colors which include spotted, bicolored and solid- colored varieties.

The non-profit organization of the International Llama Registry keeps an official genealogical system of registry and research services aimed to assist owners of the llama and its subspecies like the guanaco, vicuna and crossbreeds of their sort. The International Lama Registry lists 15 color varieties in llamas. In addition to these color variants, the AOA acknowledges four leg color patterns, 12 color patterns are solely dedicated to the neck and head of the llama and, to sum it up, twenty body color patterns. Now that is a lot of variety for any artisan or homesteader!

Chapter Two: Llamas as Pets

Here are some things you need to consider when deciding on raising a couple of llamas. Notice that we say "a couple of llamas" pretty often. This is because llamas are social animals that need the company of other farm and livestock animals to thrive. There are other things to start pondering before you actually get started on the acquisition of these beautiful animals. So let's delve into them a little more.

Chapter Two: Llamas as Pets

Before You Get One!

Baby llamas are called crias, and aren't exactly the most suitable of ages to adopt or start raising a llama. The problem with getting unweaned lama is that it grows up around you and starts treating you as if you were one of the herds. This may sound like a great way to incorporate yourself into their lives, but not so much, when you get treated like one of them and are spat on. Keep the contact with a crias to a minimum and try to wean it off the bottle by introducing solid foods when advised appropriately by a vet.

Naturally raised llamas take at least 6 months to be weaned off its mother and should gain at least half a pound to a full pound each day. Bottle-fed llamas are to be gelded much sooner than a naturally weaned llama. Give it the company of another livestock animal, preferably another lama. Seek information from knowledgeable reputable breeders or veterinarians because only they will know not to sell you an underage or unweaned crias.

Heads up! A baby llama who has not yet weaned off of its mother, should not be mistaken for a suitable pet.

Chapter Two: Llamas as Pets

Llamas need the proper amount of time to wean off its mother before being separated from it. Should you have unknowingly purchase on, you will need to do the necessary task of manually feeding it with a bottle using plain homogenized Vitamin D milk. If it doesn't gain at least a pound to a pound and a half daily, reinforce the milk with nutrients and don't cuddle it whilst feeding it.

As much as possible don't buy 'bottle babies'. Give it coarse sweet feed. Another good option is to give them quality hay early on. The llamas will start showing interest and taste it when they are ready.

Things to Remember When Keeping Llamas as Pets

Be aware! Haltered llamas are in danger of a host of unwanted accidents. It is important that any potential owner intending to raise llamas know this to avoid horrible mishaps. Owners who have not been present during the training of their llamas would leave the animals halter on, making way for all sorts of skin rashes, blisters, abscesses, calluses and ulcers. Make sure that the premises you rent or provide for your llamas have a stall or catch pen where the llamas can roam.

Make it a point to make arrangements early on to get training to train a llama because doing so will save you and your llama future challenges in terms of face to face interaction.

Do not leave your llamas harnessed whilst unattended. Don't leave them tethered to any object that can potentially injure or harm them. Too often the result of accustoming animals to a halter and leaving them tied to a tree has been a llama with a broken neck. This happens when they toss their heads to try to break free. Use an elastic extension or a bungee cord that is fast if you absolutely need to secure your llama.

The administration of vaccines as well as the giving of deworming drugs of the Lamas needs to happen on regular schedule. Crias, or baby llamas, are vaccinated before weaning between the ages of five to six months. Younger llamas tend to be more prone to parasitic diseases that can be spread from one to another through contact than the mature ones. One symptom of Coccidiosis is diarrhea. The

Chapter Two: Llamas as Pets

illness is dangerous if left undetected because it can debilitate the animal which can result to its demise.

Although deworming is still a very important part of husbandry, the bigger and more persistent problem is resistant parasites. The present recommendations now are to use de - wormer only as needed. The locale of your residency, more so, the llamas, as with the size of the herd, will greatly affect the frequency of deworming. Check fecal samples to monitor parasite loads - this is a good way to know how often you will need to deworm. Newer deworming products are also available. Check with your vet.

Lamas have been reported to choke when fed straight pellets. If you feel your lamas this way, you will likely have a case of choke especially if the animals scrimmage for their sustenance. Mix in a coarse feed with pellets. This works better than just the concentrated pellets on their own. In case of an emergency of acute choke, run a tube into the side of the llama's mouth then carefully feed the length of the pellet to it

Chapter Two: Llamas as Pets

In the event that a partially chewed pellet travels down and gets lodged in the lungs of the animal call the vet immediately. An emergency treatment with an administered antibiotic will help ward off pneumonia. Should the airways be totally obstructed, time is against you. There have been numbers of llamas that have died from asphyxiation because of half-chewed, moist pellets lodged in their throats.

Spread pellets in a wide pan to discourage episodes of choke if you do have pellets in their diet. Alternatively, put large smooth rocks in the feeding bowl so as they have to feel their way to the food, encouraging slow-feeding.

Non-breeding lamas will thrive on hay, a lush patch of land, the minerals found there and of course, fresh water to wash and cool down with.

Supplement the diet of llamas who are lactating, used for breeding or those who need to gain a bit more weight with a feed formulated especially for llamas. You can ask your vet about using goat, horse or cow formulated feed. Many llamas have been given these options without issues. However, they should not be given pellets you'd give to rabbits. These are not suitable food for your llamas.

Chapter Two: Llamas as Pets

The nutritional content of the soil where your llama is will be crucial to its everyday dietary needs. Minerals and salt is essential to the health of llamas, so, you will need to make sure that they have free access to these. These essential salts and minerals they require will also need to have selenium. You can check with your Extension Agent to find out about the selenium content of the soil of your area.

Llamas are native to the dry, thin air of the South American altiplano. They do not handle heat and humidity well. Taking care of llamas will mean that you will have to shear them in the spring. They will also need to be cooled down with water, especially in the belly and rear end where it can get really hot. You will have provided your llamas shelter from direct sun. You will also need to fashion some kind of air movement if they have an enclosed shelter.

Chapter Two: Llamas as Pets

Chapter Three: Getting Acquainted with Llamas

An animal that displays laborious breathing is in trouble. This is a sign of distress most especially during the hot summer months of the year. A llama who was recently in a wrangle with another llama or one who had been recently spat on would typically display this manner of breathing, however, in a rested state this is to be treated as an unusual manner of breathing for a llama. Whenever you notice this, deduce that the llamas suffering from heat stress make sure to take immediate measures to cool them down

Chapter Three: Getting Acquainted with Llamas

all over. You will notice males display engorged testicles when they are in heat distress.

You will want to take note of the proper body temperature of your farm animals to avoid running the risk of undetected infections. The correct healthy temperature of an adult llama is a hundred degrees. If its body temp reads 103 and above, be alarmed and grab the hose for a long and purposed water down. Make sure that you shear your llamas during springtime.

Be aware of poisonous plants and trees in the area perimeter the llamas are allowed to roam. Lamas are casual eaters and dine one a number of food sorts. There are a number of plants and foliage which can be harmful to them when ingested. Some of these plants are rhododendron and also wilted cherry prove to be lethal to llamas. Remember to check with your extension agent and other associations concerned about camelid care. These are the individuals you want to be in contact with because they will be able to give you vital knowledge on the care of llamas.

Chapter Three: Getting Acquainted with Llamas

Lamas need their own sort for company, so it will be likely that you will have to purchase two or more to keep your animals happy. And even in a paired situation, responsible purchasers and raisers of llamas have come into some sort of trouble at one point or another, be on your toes. A paired llama will find it uncomfortable and out of order to be separated from the other. Make sure that you have a companion, responsible as you and trained to handle the animal when you take them for short walks.

A llama left behind can be cause for agitation of the one being left or the one leaving the other. There have been situations when the llama left behind would try to hop outside in an attempt to go along for the walk. Keep in mind that even in a herd situation, llamas display utter concern for the one being separated from the rest.

The shelter and fencing requirement for llamas will need to be ideal for your animals: They will need some sort of protection from the elements like strong winds, snow, rain, lightning, and sun. You should be able to provide proper shelter for them to avert any untoward, jumpy behavior. Make sure that the barricade you construct for

Chapter Three: Getting Acquainted with Llamas

your animals are sturdy and adequate. For obvious reasons, barbed wire is not a good fencing material since llamas are curious animals that can get into all sorts of tight space where they shouldn't be. The barbs that poke out through the wires can easily cause injury their big eyes, or scratch its skin.

Do not mix in females with almost year-old males and vice versa; young females are not to reside in close quarters with males. Llamas are somewhat precocious, and they get fertile at quite an early age; therefore it is possible for females to get pregnant after four months. A young male by the sixth month will be able to coerce an adult female to ovulate. Some of these young guns may even be persuasive enough to mount and penetrate the female. Llamas are animals and do not understand the impacts of incest. Most especially under the controlled confinement situation, they will not have the faculties to understand or distinguish family from non-relatives. Natural mechanisms and trigger - signal occurs in the wild, but not so in confinement.

You will have to make sure to learn how to file down the teeth of the male llama. When they reach the age of two

Chapter Three: Getting Acquainted with Llamas

years old their teeth would have also matured with great potential to cause harm to another male in the brood. This is to be taken to heart most especially in pens where males who breed are kept. You will have to have some sort of avoidance of injury or heat stress. A male can get fixated and might run after a rival, even in 100 degree weather, till he collapses. Discuss how to remove tips of your pet's fighting teeth with your veterinarian.

Make sure to provide a chute or a safe restraint you will need for the task of trimming and cutting down the llama's toenails. Uncut toenails that are left to grow become cumbersome for the llama to deal with. Not trimming its nails may lead to rendering it lame. You will also need the chute for when vaccine need to be administered to the animal. It will also be handy for quarantine purposes when the animal is injured or recuperating from an illness. It also gives them a space to rest when in the process of healing.

If you are not a farm person to begin with but have the passion and desire to raise livestock and farm animals, you will need to learn how to deal with everyday dealings as well as routine stuff and other emergency incidents. When

Chapter Three: Getting Acquainted with Llamas

you have a pregnant llama that is ready to give birth, you will need to be mindful and observant of the animal. Once hard labor or active pushing has commenced a nose or a foot should appear at some point. Ideally, one or the other should start to show sooner.

Prolonged labor is neither natural nor safe for the mother llama. Should the llama lie on one side or another, prior to active pushing, if it gets up and lays down, if the mother llama lays on her belly with her head tilted on its side get in touch with your vet immediately. Ideally, your vet should be on hand or at least aware of the expected date of delivery. If you don't have a vet, and this is not advisable, at all, you should make it a point to learn all you will need to know on what is expected of you. You will have to make sure that you know what you are getting into, the amount of time and work needed from you and the procedures you will need to undertake when caring for llamas.

Colostrum and plasma will be very important for the newborn crias when it emerges. Unfortunately, some new mom's will not have milk or it will be produced too slowly for the needs of the new and vulnerably weak baby llama.

Chapter Three: Getting Acquainted with Llamas

Some new newborn llamas are weak. There is nothing sadder than a llama owner calling around to distant lama neighbors at midnight in search of life-saving colostrum.

Colostrum is the yellowish first milk, which needs to be given to a baby within around twelve hours after birth. Colostrum helps ensure the young llamas healthy future with the transference of vital colostrum to the baby, and to give it strength. Don't wait until the last hour! Make it a point to have at a quart up to a gallon of colostrum from a goat or cow, frozen in 6 or 8 ounce freezer bags or containers. Make sure that the colostrum you freeze prior to the birth.

Harvest the colostrum from cows or goats that have been vaccinated. Make sure that you have a little feeding box complete with the tools you will need to feed the colostrum to the newborn crias. Make sure that you test these implements prior to usage to make sure that they both work. When deep frozen, colostrum will keep for a long time; keep at least 2 liters of this frozen.

Chapter Three: Getting Acquainted with Llamas

Llamas are browsers and naturally curious beings that will inspect and get their noses into things where they shouldn't. However, they don't know any better, and will satisfy their curiosity if given enough objects in their pen to inspect. Do not leave anything around in or hanging near their pens which they can get hold of or are within reach. Keep objects in the pens at a minimum. Do not leave anything that will pose danger to the llamas under your care. Keep away, brooms, tractor or motor parts, bailing string, wheelbarrows, lumber and wire away from your animals. Make it a point to have some tools, parts, equipment and objects you use in another structure. Make sure that you keep any objects they can chew on, or get tangled in.

Chapter Four: Some Facts about Llamas

The Llama is not a small animal, standing tall at 40 to 50 inches high at the withers and 60 to 72 inches tall at the poll; they generally weigh around 18 to 31 pounds at birth. They ideally weigh around 250 to 300 pounds upon full maturity. Female llamas reach their mature size at two years of age. Males take half a year more and mature at 3 years old. The average lifespan of llamas approximately range from 20 to 25 years, sometimes longer if given optimum care.

Chapter Four: Some Facts about Llamas

Aside from the useful traits of the llama as a farm animal, they also have another useful feature that if utilized thoughtfully, could be a small passive income. The fur of llamas have long been used to make yarn which are in turn woven into rugs, helping keep the homes and residents of the higher Andes snug and warm. These products manufactured using the fiber of the llama comes in a variety of thickness, density and grades. The fineness of the thread quality largely depends on the area of the animal the fiber is taken.

The fiber produced by the llama not only keeps the animal insulated from the elements, it also makes for some of the best thread to make stick rugs, and heavy-duty bags. Let's get to know llamas a little more and get a clear picture of their general traits and attributes.

Appearance

The camelids possess long, graceful necks. The llama has a relatively small head, covered in finer hair, with the most adorably large peepers. On the temples of their

Chapter Four: Some Facts about Llamas

smallish heads are large curved (ideally) banana-shaped ears. Wool of 3 to 8 inches covers their body in a variety of colours and shades. Short hair covers the underside and legs of the llamas and the lengthier wool can be found in the neck, back and general body area of this magnificent beast.

The wool that covers the llama's body purposes as nature's way of protecting the llama from the elements of nature. The llama's wool is thick and dense enough to withstand the cold, gales of wind, snow and rain. The shorter hairs covering the underbelly and the head of the llama allows the animal to dissipate heat during the warmer seasons or when they are located in warmer regions. The wool of the lama does not possess lanolin (a component present in sheep wool) which helps water resistance. It has a pretty long tail that measure up to 12 inches once the llama matures.

Characteristics

When fearful or angered, a llama makes a distinct groaning sound. When the llama goes "mwa" it most likely is

Chapter Four: Some Facts about Llamas

trying to call attention and signaling danger. It could also make this noise when angered by other animals or humans around it. So, beware. You will know the level of anxiety of the llama when it lays back its ears on its head. Level of agitation of the animal may also be measured by the materials mingled in the spit.

Just like most other animals of the wild, llamas emits "orgle" sounds during the mating season and when the sexually aroused llama is ready to mate. The sound the male llama makes sounds much like gargling, although with a more forceful edge to it making a sound closely sounding a gargling buzz. One would notice this sound being made by an aroused male during mating season. This would carry on throughout the deed of mating and can last anywhere from 15 minutes to an hour.

Given the proper training, the llama will be socialized to humans and other animals, making spitting a rare occurrence. However, do not be surprised if you see them spitting at each other. Llamas move ranks in a herd. They can attain better herd-rank out of small victories in fights, so

Chapter Four: Some Facts about Llamas

their place in the herd is never static. This is typically settled between males to determine who ranks up to alpha status.

These fights between two contending males can become visually dramatic with a lot of spitting and rough wrangling. They would be seen ramming at each other using their chests. They would be seen kicking each other and wrestling with their necks, with intention on tripping the other and knocking its opponent off balance.

While males would be the one mostly seen in fights mentioned, females would only see spitting at other herd members as a means of controlling them. The social structure of a herd of llamas is almost fluid with the changes in rank and is never static, but they do live lives much like a family would, taking care of each other and watching out for the rest. When something is amiss with the territory or if there is some sort of threat detected by one, it would set of a warning with a bray signaling and alerting others.

Chapter Four: Some Facts about Llamas

Behavior

Llamas have been historically mingled with people so, they are very social animals who require the interaction of other animals of similar docility as well as humans. When properly socialized, they are great companions who display calmness and gentleness. They are truly fun to hang out with because they are just as interested in humans as humans are to them. They are extremely curious and most will approach people easily. Llamas are well-socialized, very friendly and pleasant to be around.

On the other hand, there is such a thing as over-socializing a llama. It's been observed that a bottle-fed cria (what a baby llama is called) and one which is over-handled as young llamas will grow up to be harder to handle because you, the owner, would be considered part of their own, and may tend to treat other humans as they would treat each other - which is to say, spit at them. So it is highly advisable to keep contact during this bottle-feeding time to a minimum, and that they cease as early as possible.

Chapter Four: Some Facts about Llamas

They may have a bad rap because of all the spitting they have been captured on film doing, but in truth, spitting is more typical amongst and between llamas than it is to humans. Llamas spit in order to put other llamas of the herd in place, or between two contending males. Spitting at humans only happens when the llamas becomes agitated by the humans interacting with them. Spitting is primarily a defense mechanism they employ when they feel threatened and may occur if the llamas are very poorly socialized.

Llamas are great sound producers, making a variety of sounds depending on situation and season. When upset, anxious or threatened, llamas make a sound much like braying, giving signal to other llamas in the herd of possible, imminent danger. During mating season, llamas make a low, almost like a buzzing, gurgling sound which can go on for the duration of the mating session

Chapter Four: Some Facts about Llamas

Chapter Five: Requirements When Raising Llamas

Just the mere fact that llamas come from the high plains of the Andes, gives us an idea of the vast open spaces to which it is truly accustomed. And with llamas growing up to be close to 400 lbs., they are not tiny, at all. Being the herd animals they are they are smart packing beasts that thrive best amongst their own or similar-tempered animals. All of these characteristics and features of the llama gives us a pretty clear idea of the space it would need if you do decide to get one or two. Remember that llamas are animals that

Chapter Five: Requirements When Raising Llamas

need others like them. They need to be around other llamas, they may tend to become lonely and depressed.

Requirements

Llamas are like other farm animals. Just like other farm animals, llamas will need a lot of outdoor space where they can run around, stretch their legs and be in contact with other farm animals. They need a fenced in area where they can do what llamas do and have the safety of an enclosure to avoid them from wandering off too far from their safe haven. Just like other farm animals, and because their fur is not water resistant, they would need a barn area where they can duck into when the weather gets to inhospitable for outside play. They need plenty of fenced outdoor space, along with a barn area to hang out in when it's cold or rainy.

That is not reason to stop you though. You can in fact own several if you are located anywhere near a farm who facilitates the stay of large farm animals kept as pets by owners who do not have the necessary space these magnificent beast need. There are existing farms who take in livestock, farm animals. For a stipulated monthly fee to

Chapter Five: Requirements When Raising Llamas

cover lodging and food, individuals may secure a great space for suitable for lodging, grazing, and playing for your pet llamas. However, most stipulations on these agreements state that you are to be responsible for the grooming and tending of the general needs of the llamas under your ownership.. You are to be responsible for the training, upkeep and vet care costs of the animals. The setup of paying for farm lodging for your livestock and farm pets gives them the much needed space and company they require in order to get a rounder social structure. We'll be talking about the maintenance of male lamas with a bit more detail later.

Llamas will require frequent and regular grooming. They will need to have their fur sheared and their toenails trimmed. Their fleece will need to be shown at least once a year. They are a hardy sort but will need to follow a vaccine schedule designed by a veterinarian which should be based on the potential disease threats in the area.

Llamas create less fibre as compared to their cousins, the alpacas, and the fleece of the llama is of generally lesser quality. Llamas were bred for other, more robust-work

Chapter Five: Requirements When Raising Llamas

purposes. Good quality llama fleece is hard to find therefore there is a lot of potential in growing a llama fleece industry.

Necessities

Llamas are fairly easy to raise as long as you get the proper initial training and insights to its successful care. You will also need a team of people in the background ready to jump to the call of the care f your pet llamas. It takes a little under a village to raise these magnificent beasts of beauty and charm. Make sure that you have a vet you can reach at any time needed, and that they, too, have contingency plans for when they are unavailable. Llamas have a tendency to some parasitic organisms and need the regular checkup and husbandry of a vet on a monthly basis to make sure that they are healthy.

Apart from the routine check - ups, you should be covered for any untoward and unforeseen instances. As much as you try to take all necessary precautions and caution, llamas will get into some sort of situation that would deem emergency vet care. Injuries to these animals,

Chapter Five: Requirements When Raising Llamas

especially in the fore and hind quarter areas, should never be ignored and must have an expert's consult and advice. Limb injuries can be fatal to other livestock as with llamas. Because they do not understand that injury would deem them to rest, they would go on ahead limping about until the condition gets worse. Injured livestock need to take a rest and need the guidance and care of humans at a time as such.

Being in the vicinity of an animal hospital will also be something you will want to tick off your list or at least, knowing where to call and who when and if the need arises.

The beauty of securing your llamas a place in a nearby farm allows them to be able to (aside from the food you will be providing them) be fed on pasture. Make sure that you pay a careful visit to the farm you intend to put your llamas up for board. Make yourself aware of the plants and grazing areas they are allowed to wander to. There are poisonous plants that can be very toxic and deadly to your llamas and you wouldn't want to risk a very sick llama on your hands. The heartbreak would be regrettable and too late.

Chapter Five: Requirements When Raising Llamas

As long as the pasture is free from poisonous flora, hay along with complete rations, are acceptable meals that can be readily within reach for your friendly and sturdy llamas. The sort of feed available as well as what should be fed your llamas will vary by area. Apart from these needs they will also need vitamins and supplements which you will need to discuss with the vet you choose to work with. You may also look for an agriculture extension specialist who can help in the maintenance of your llamas.

Depending on the area you live, weather will play a big factor in the shelter needs of the llamas you take under your care. The weather of the region of your residence (or the llamas) will clearly play a factor in shelter needs. A barn would be the best place to house llamas located in colder regions. Where the climate is warmer, llamas may be housed in three-sided barns. An open roofed area would be the required housing for llamas in really hot weather since this would allow for more effective airflow throughout the structure. The important bit to remember is the animals need to have their own enclosures to themselves.

Chapter Five: Requirements When Raising Llamas

They should be separated from each other and given their personal space. The fences are meant to keep them away from farm dogs as well. Llamas need to be around their sort, so it is most likely that you will get a pair of llamas at the very least. You may choose to get a same sex pair, unless your intention is to breed them later.

Now would be a good time for you to ask yourself if you are ready for the responsibilities of owning and raising a couple of llamas. Raising them would not only require time but considerable annual amount for vet care. Not only will you have to work a schedule that would include the frequent visits to the farm, you would also have to factor in the necessity of the regular checkups they need.

Llamas are generally hardy animals that with proper care, are easy to raise. As with other animals you may have taken in, you will want to discover the possible illness and diseases llamas are prone to in order to identify and avoid these conditions from happening or progressing in the animal under your guardianship. We hall go over a list of health concerns a llama could experience. It may seem they are prone to quite a bit of hosts. However, being properly

Chapter Five: Requirements When Raising Llamas

informed as an owner and caregiver, you will be at a better advantage of caring properly for them.

Keep in mind that having a vet you can call on and one who can perform the monthly check ups of the animals will help prevent many of these maladies. The llama is one of the most versatile animals around and is great companions to boot with a host of great talents you will be surprised to learn. Regular vet care will ensure that you and your llamas will enjoy a long relationship.

Chapter Six: Health Concerns and Care

Llamas are hardy animals that thrive well in a pair or a herd, best. They are grazing animals that can get most of their sustenance from the plants and foliage of the area they occur. In captivity, llamas can benefit from a farm-style setting where they can graze, wander and have free range of the natural plant feedings available. It is imperative that you speak to your extension specialist. It is important that this individual is present to inspect the soundness of the area's foliage. The sort of feed will be different for every area. You will need to discuss supplementing your llama's food with vitamins and minerals.

Chapter Six: Health Concerns and Care

Tips When Feeding and Caring For Llamas

Make sure that the llamas always have fresh water because this is going to be vital to the wellbeing of your llamas.

Your llamas will need appropriate fencing to keep them within limits. It is crucial to have a space where the llamas are together but are separated by suitable barriers. It is imperative to the safety of the animals that you keep away from their reach any implements, tools, equipment, parts, wires, bail strings, lumber and metal sheets that can topple over. Anything that will pose some sort of danger or another to animals should be kept out of their shed and barn. These should at the very least be kept at a corner of the barn where they are away and far from the curious animals in the barn.

Be sure that you are aware of the typical weather patterns of the area of where the animal will be staying. Their sheds and barns need to be suitable for the prevalent weather conditions of the region. As much as llamas of the Andes are able to thrive and exist with no issues with just a few trees to duck under, it is still up to you as their keeper to provide appropriate shelter for the magnificent beasts. Make

Chapter Six: Health Concerns and Care

sure that the farm will be able to provide enough water for cleaning and rehydrating purposes. Water is life in a big way, no matter how easily we take it for granted. The body temperature of a llama can shoot to an alarming 103 degrees and you will need to take measures during the warmer season to keep the llamas cooled. Since their fur does not contain the lanolin that sheep's fur does, llamas are not waterproof. They will need suitable shelter when the rains come.

They are one of the most versatile of animals that not only possess a calm demeanor about them (if properly trained and socialized); they are also utilitarian in so many ways. The contributions they have imparted to the humans they interact with are astounding. Lauded to be the new dogs of livestock animals, llamas are such friendly, docile and loyal pets, but don't expect them to play fetch with you. Let's look at some of the more common ailments that llamas are susceptible to. Keep in mind that this is in no way intended to replace the advice of a medical expert. There is a very thorough list of a host of ills that can plague llamas, making it look they are prone to lots of ills. However, llamas

Chapter Six: Health Concerns and Care

are quite hardy and they do quite well when proper veterinary care is sought early on in the event of something going wrong.

Regular veterinary care will be required and may be expensive if health problems arise. You can't expect to recognize every single thing, but you are expected, as a responsible caretaker of llamas, to be able to identify when something is amiss with any one of your llama wards. You will also need the expertise of a medical expert,

Common Illnesses

Abscess

An abscess is an infection after an injury is sustained. It is a pocket of pus made up of dead tissue cells created by the body as a way to fight infection. When this happens, dirt or a splinter of wood can enter the skin from the puncture wound. Abscess look like an angry, fluid filled pocket of skin that can be painful when touched. It would feel either hot or cold to the touch. When the abscess is full, the skin

Chapter Six: Health Concerns and Care

will burst, allowing for the release of the pus. If the abscess does not burst it may need some coaxing through lancing the localized area.

An abscess can be quite painful. You can help out your llama by cleaning it. Start by washing your hands clean and gloving up. Proceed to clip away at the wool around the area of the abscess. Using a cotton ball drenched in Betadine, gently clean the area. You can either scar the utmost of the abscess mound with a lancet or a needle from a syringe. Express the pus then wash the area with hydrogen peroxide. Clean this area on a daily basis with hydrogen peroxide. Make sure that you dress the wound after you clean it and change this every day until you see the area start to scab.

Once it starts scabbing don't cover the wound up too tightly - just enough that it does not get any dirt on the area. Ask your vet about prepared-gauze that not only protects the abscess from getting infected again, it also fights off the infection, treating it even after the cleaning process. Bacteria from pus are infectious to humans who come into contact with it from an open wound. Make sure that you wear gloves, it's just hygienic.

Chapter Six: Health Concerns and Care

Bare Nose

Owners have often spotted bare areas on the bridge of their llama wards. These bare spots on the noses of the animals become even more common during the summer months when flies are prevalent. The bare spots could be brought about by the llama rubbing that particular spot during the hot months. Nose spots could also be due to the winter dryness. You could help along the situation by applying a little bit of Vaseline on the spot. You may also try alternating petroleum jelly with Zinc ointment, vitamin E oil or Preparation H.

Berserk Male Syndrome

Berserk Male Syndrome is an aggressive behavior which male llamas may experience when they reach a couple of years old. Some male llamas display this at an even younger age. It is mainly caused by humans who have over-handled when the male llamas were young. This syndrome can also be brought about by prolonged bottle feeding. The male llama perceives humans as their peers. This is why it is important to follow the rule of thumb when bottle-feeding a young crias. Llamas who spend more time bonding with humans rather than other llamas will become very territorial.

Blue Eye Syndrome

There seems to be an association with blue-eyes and deafness in llamas. Deafness is a known disorder amongst llamas and their cousins, the alpacas. The cause of this condition is not known, but time and observation has shown the association of deafness to blue - eyed llamas. This is especially true for llamas with blue eyes and a coat of white fleece. Hyperpigmentation and deafness is a combination that is not uncommon to other species, such as canines, felines or even humans, however there is little known about this combination of characteristics that ties it to deafness.

Drooping Eye

There are llamas that tend to display the drooping eye syndrome when they feel stress. It could also be a genetic condition passed on from parents to crias, so it could

Chapter Six: Health Concerns and Care

actually be a trait passed on. Therefore, make sure to be observant to discover what happens before the episode of the drooping eye, if it is something you notice on occasion.

Digestive System

The llama has one of the most unique and interesting digestive systems consisting of a special stomach that has separate compartments. When they eat, the food passes through the esophagus and it then rests in the rumen, which is the first compartment of the llama's stomach. The llamas would then regurgitate the eaten food only to chew it again. If you look closely at an eating llama, you will notice them regurgitating their food and would actually be able to see the lump of food, or cud, traveling back up the neck of the llama. Once back in their mouth, the llama would then chew the food again between fifty to seventy times in a figure-eight motion and would swallow the cud again. They would then wait for about eight seconds, to half-regurgitate another and munch on it. Once the cud is re-swallowed, this would then pass into the two other stomach compartments of the

Chapter Six: Health Concerns and Care

llamas stomach. The rumination process the llama performs allows it to break down the food it ingests efficiently.

Fighting Teeth

Male llamas will grow massive teeth which you will need to learn to file down. The male llamas will grow these fighting teeth at approximately two years of age. These teeth can be very dangerous to them and other males when mixed together. The fighting teeth of the male llamas be dealt with using a special wire and a little anesthesia.

Heat Stress

Llamas, being that they come from the high punas of the Andes, require attention in when raised in warmer regions. Make it a point to provide water they can drink from at any given time. You will also need to provide them with a shaded area, and out from under the sun. Long fleeced animals, like the llama, will have to be sheared. Cool down the llama's legs and belly with a hose. You could also set out a child's wading pool where they can sit in. Give

Chapter Six: Health Concerns and Care

them a bucket of water with electrolytes. Feed your llamas with the recommended diet for easier digestion.

Good nutrition is very crucial during the hot months of the year. If you plan to breed them, breed and birth them during the cooler months of the year. Indications of heat stress in llamas include drooling, open-mouth breathing, they may drooping their lower lip, stagger, an unable to stand another sign of heat stress is lack or absence of appetite. A temperature of over 103 degrees is a danger sign. Measures to lower the body of the animal should be immediately carried out. Monitor the llama you suspect of heat stress.

Lice

There are 2 kinds of lice, and you will recognize these pests as tiny wingless insects that can be harmful to a llama; one is the sucking louse can cause your llama to develop anemia.

Lice spread amongst animals through direct contact. Indications of lice manifest by the infected llama scratching.

Chapter Six: Health Concerns and Care

You will want to inspect your animals for these kinds of parasite especially around winter time when the llamas are typically housed together in close quarters. Treatment for the sucking lice is injectable or fenthion pour on (Tiguvon) applied topically at the shoulder blades.

The biting louse is usually white or tan in color. These bugs can be found on the surface of the skin. The biting louse can be found on the llama's neck, face, thighs, and tail. The usual treatments of lice is a pour - on medication like Ivomec SQ. Use a mixture of 50% Methoxychlor or 50% Rose Dust, which is applied topically.

Lump on Jaw

You may occasionally notice a hard bump develop on your llama's cheek and along the jawline. It could *merely be a* nice, big chunk of cud in their cheek. However, it could also be an indication of an abscess. It could also be a tooth problem; therefore you will need to investigate further. This is a good time to remind new, potential owners to get their

Chapter Six: Health Concerns and Care

own training covered before making any payments on these animals.

Mange

Mange is a skin disease common in Llamas that's also contagious. It is transferred through direct contact with a diseased animal. An animal can also be by contaminated, indirectly, through quarters or dust baths. The mite's life cycle which is around 2 to 3 weeks is lived out on the animal. The Sarcoptic mange is caused specifically by Sarcoptes scabiei. These mites burrow under the llama's legs, belly, and ears. The affected area will then develop bald spots, crusts, and also flaking. It has a leather-like feel as the condition progresses. You should check with your veterinarian.

Meningeal Worm

This larva would penetrate ground snails which could be eaten by llamas whilst they are in pasture. The larvae of the parasite would thrive along the nervous system

Chapter Six: Health Concerns and Care

of the animal and the brain causing the llama damage to its central nervous system. Unfortunately, there isn't any definitive way to diagnose Meningeal Worm. However, sometimes symptoms can be treated effectively. Some of the most common symptoms of this imbalance are shown signs of weakness when attempting to walk. Observe the suspected infected llama for slow weight loss. Treatments include multiple doses of a de – wormer.

Ringworm

This is usually identified because of a bald spot on the animal. The affected area is manifested by crusty lesions. Ringworms is a fungal growth. You can apply iodine to the affected skin area of the animal as treatment. Your vet can confirm the presence of ringworm via a microscopic exam. This is contagious to other animals as well as people. Make sure that you either use gloves or immediately wash your hands thoroughly after treatment.

Chapter Six: Health Concerns and Care

Toenails

Toenail trimming will be an important bit of responsibility you will need to accomplish on a regular basis. Make sure that you schedule time for this grooming procedure, most especially if you are getting more than a pair of them. The frequency will greatly depend on each animal. It would also depend on the surface which they frequently walk.

Llamas working the trails will probably require trimming less often than those who are on soft pasture all the time.. Trim down the sides of the nail even with the pad in two or three cuts or depending on the need, then cut across the point.

Take care not to cut too far or it will most certainly bleed, and this will be painful. Cutting too deep into the quick could infect that area of the llama, since they are on their feet most of the time. When you lift the leg to trim the nails, make sure that you lift the foot straight back and bend it normally. Do not pull the leg out to the side because this will make the task even more cumbersome.

Chapter Six: Health Concerns and Care

Vaccinations

You will want to make it a point to vaccinate your llamas every year with (CD/T). You will need to consult your vet for the proper dosage. A good time to vaccinate your llamas is in the spring just before the weather gets too hot. You should not vaccinate any pregnant llamas breeding or breeding ones in the 60 day period after. Another booster vaccination must also be administered mother llamas given 60 days before it gives birth. You will also need to vaccinate a crias with CD/T between its 10-12 weeks. Give it another booster shot of CD/T 4 weeks after the first one administered.

Chapter Six: Health Concerns and Care

Chapter Seven: Husbandry Practices for Llamas

For such a big animal, llamas actually eat very little. Not only is their staple food economical, it can be sustained with foliage and plants available around the farm. Llamas are browsers; therefore they will not eat from one plant alone. Make it a point to coordinate with your environmental agent because you will want them to inspect the plants growing around the area. The llama is one of the camelid commonly found in farms. It is a long, lanky animal with long necks. They have the general body shape of a

Chapter Seven: Husbandry Practices for Llamas

camel. They weigh about 300-400 lbs. and have banana shaped ears. They have long thick fur typically around their necks and legs.

They like to stay in herds and travel with a trusted and calm buddy. This is important to note, because llamas don't do well on their own. Some new owners start out with a couple to a few llamas on the onset of their commitment to raise the animals. Others who have only kept one have found that keeping them in the company of other like-sized and like-tempered animals can do the work as well. But nothing beats having the llamas under your care to feel the security and safety amongst their sort, in numbers.

There will be basic husbandry skills which you will need to learn in order for them to live a well-rounded, properly socialized life under your care and guidance. We shall go over some of the more important aspects of taking care of the needs that your llamas will be requiring. You will also have to learn many of these through experiences and from the individual animals who will be under your care.

Chapter Seven: Husbandry Practices for Llamas

Haltering

Haltering is a basic trait that must be taught to each of the llamas in your herd. There are a few simple, and tested, concepts of easy haltering that will help you attain your goal for the llama and, ultimately, yourself. We shall talk about and cover one of the more traditional methods of haltering your llama.

And since llamas are easily trainable haltering skills, as long as they are effectively carried out, can be taught at any age of the llama. When you train the animal is not nearly as critical as where and how you train your llamas. So, if you had not been able to train your llamas after they wean, you still have time to do it. First thing's first, you will need to set up a consistent are for training. Fashion their training area to be easily navigable. Give your llama ample time to settle in on its own. Once it is at ease, start by gently talking to your llama. This not only very important for the bonding process between you and your llama, talking to it will help it build trust in you, In addition, talking the animal will help it learn words you use.

Chapter Seven: Husbandry Practices for Llamas

Begin the training on haltering in an enclosure with a dimension of about 10′ x 10′. Stand quietly until it is comfortable sharing the space with you when it accepts your presence as a non-threat then start moving closer. If it makes any moves, stop, and immediately tell it to "stand." The llama has to learn through verbal cues accompanied by gestures.

A typical mistake new caregivers make is utter the stay command whilst the llama is in motion, making it relate the act of moving about with the command "stand."

Your goal is to get closer to your llama. When you have achieved this, you may go ahead and offer it your hand to it. Stroke the llama on the neck as he stands still. Your aim is to put your dominant arm around the llama's neck without it moving or pulling away from you. If the llama does pull away, so should you release the pressure. The more you pull, even more so will the llama pull. Always try to release when the llama is not pulling away from you. Along with verbal cues, or commands, don't forget to use your verbal rewards and acknowledgements. Once your

Chapter Seven: Husbandry Practices for Llamas

llama is standing still, gently talk to him, pet it on the neck and then release him.

Keep It Short - Sessions

Consider the age of the llama as this will be crucial to the success of training it properly. During training it is important for you to allot the length of each training session. Just like children, llamas have a short attention span, so do not run the risk of frustration on either you or the llama.

Make it a point to catch the llama you are training to halter as described here for several days in a row. Have consecutive training sessions, rather than long, sporadic ones. Haltering the llama serves you and other individuals who have to work on the upkeep of its health.

It is important to just train the llama with catch and release at the onset of your training. Haltering it only when it has to go the vet may have the llama be weary of the catch and halter process.

The next step after you are able to catch your llama is to next work on desensitizing its nose for the haltering process. You want to wrap your dominant forearm around the llama then run your other hand up its neck to its cheek. Once you have achieved this, stroke its nose. Your progress during this step of training will greatly depend on how your llama reacts to the action. Make sure to do this for about three to four times then end the lesson.

Fits is Important

A proper fitting halter will be essential and necessary when you are confident about haltering. You don't want to start the haltering process only to discover that you can't fit the halter over its nose.

- Stand with your hip into your llama's shoulder (flanking each other from shoulder to hip) whilst both you and the llama face the same direction. Hold the halter in one hand.

- Then put your dominant arm around the llama's neck, mindful to be gentle

Chapter Seven: Husbandry Practices for Llamas

- Raise your dominant hand, or the one holding the halter, with deliberate upward speed, making sure that it is parallel with the neck, and just a tad under the chin.

It's a Matter of Trust

Put the halter on then hen remove it. Practice these moves a few times to get used to the movements. Again, the time you will need to accomplish this training task will depend on largely on the llama's reaction. It's just sound to practice catching, haltering, and releasing.

During the first and second sessions, you merely want to show the llama that the whole process poses no threat and is not a big deal. As soon as the llama accepts these procedures with no adverse reactions, carry on.

Chapter Seven: Husbandry Practices for Llamas

Buckled

Once you do fasten the buckle of the halter allow the llama to get used to how it feels. Make sure you get it a halter that fits. One that fits properly will not work up into its eyes.

You want to avoid chasing your llama around when working with it. This causes stress to the llama. That kind of atmosphere just makes it more challenging to create a positive atmosphere for learning. Since this time of training is crucial for both you and your llama, make sure you create a space that is conducive to it. You will have to limit your llama's movements by placing the llama being trained for haltering in a smaller pen. Not only will it teach your llama to stand calmly in a space with you, this also allows for a closer interaction.

At this time, it will be easy to be tempted to use bribes or treats to get desired response and results from the llama. We urge you to do this at the very minimal and withdraw these unnecessary coercions. You will, after all, need to accomplish haltering your animals on a fairly regular basis and you will not want to have to resort to urging them

Chapter Seven: Husbandry Practices for Llamas

through bribery each time. Ultimately, your goal is to halter the llama with minimal stress, for you and your llama using a crutch or a bribe will make it a harder to get rid of later.

Practice safety for both you and the animals. Halter training is to be done one llama at a time in a small pen. Keep in mind that a llama, no matter how old they are extremely strong beasts. Instead of exerting force, keep your cool during training and create a calm atmosphere for the learning process of haltering.

Resistance

This is a time to build trust toward each other. This will greatly come in handy, most notably for when you introduce new and what may be scary things for the animal. The animal may show resistance by raising its nose to avoid being haltered. It may fling the halter off just before you get it buckled. They may just go off running away when you remove it or run away from you the minute they spot the halter in your hand. It will be up to you to create a calm

Chapter Seven: Husbandry Practices for Llamas

space for learning and it will be up to you to teach your llama that haltering need not be unpleasant.

Slow Your Hands Down

You will need to be observant of each of your llama's body language. Be prepared for reactions you have seen in the past. You will be able to sense the tension in the animal. You will be able to tell if the animal flings its head. It will be up to you to keep a calm demeanor, and take it slow. Speak to it in gentle tones. Keep the pressure adequate when releasing the halter and practice releasing it as fast as you can without harm to the animal or yourself.

Remember to take control when you unbuckle, and before you remove the halter. Keep in mind the past experiences during this time of release. Start slowly, and gradually gain control of the animal after you have unbuckled it from the halter. Eventually, you will succeed in release the llama whilst retaining control over it.

Chapter Seven: Husbandry Practices for Llamas

The rate of your progress is related directly to style and method of training. Most llamas can learn and get used to the process of catching and haltering. They are usually able to become familiar with these before you actually go on to the next progression.

Chapter Seven: Husbandry Practices for Llamas

Chapter Eight: Barn Maintenance and Litter Boxes

Experienced llama owners have observed and known that llamas use communal spaces. They use communal piles, and more often than not these piles come in multiple numbers, but all are communal, nonetheless. What most people don't know is that llamas can learn to use litter boxes, making it easier for the caregivers to clean up after the llamas. Potty training the llamas under your care helps maintain cleanliness in the barn.

Chapter Eight: Barn Maintenance and Litter Boxes

Most experienced llamas owners have discovered this trait in the llamas and litter boxes has been part of barn fixtures for many years. This poop management equipment is a time saver.

The Litter Box

Any llama owner would want to work smart and not hard, to keep things running smoothly in their little piece of heaven on earth. There is no reason for a new llama owner to have to go through the tedious process of going from one dung pile to another to collect manure. Manure management for llamas can be different from other livestock animals, or even horses. Hay can assist in soaking up urine but is quite inefficient in the long run and it also tends to magnify the stink of the urine making the odor worse. Although sand can be beneficial in the warmer months since it can be hosed to lower the animal's body temperature. However, it can be a backbreaking task to move the sand. Sand also gets buried deep in the skin of the llamas, making it harder to clean them off during bath time.

Chapter Eight: Barn Maintenance and Litter Boxes

Pine shavings seem to work great because it soaks up urine, and will keep the barn smelling good. But don't be surprised if your llamas kick and track litter all over the place. With this in mind you can now navigate through the barn and start figuring out which corner is best to use as their communal area to do nature's business.

Litter Training Your Llamas

- Scatter shavings in the general area where they usually go. The shavings or sawdust will absorb the urine.

- Replace the soiled shavings with a fresh batch each time after cleaning it.

- When you start noticing the llamas "going" on the shavings you put, and you are happy with the spot, you can now think about constructing the retaining

Chapter Eight: Barn Maintenance and Litter Boxes

walls, which is pretty much a low wall, ideally set at a well - ventilated corner of the barn.

- Do this by creating a low wall (roughly a few inches higher than ankle-level.

- Fill in the area four inches deep with shavings or sawdust.

- Up to as many as four llamas can use this box at one time including babies who quickly mimic the toilet habits of their mama's.

- The smallest box you can use would roughly be an area of 3 inches by 6 inches. This works well with small clusters of llamas, about one to four of them at a time. This means you will have to have more potty areas if you have more than a couple of llamas. The biggest can go up to 8 inches by 8 inches and would take two hauls of shavings.

Chapter Eight: Barn Maintenance and Litter Boxes

- You will notice that the animals will recognize the odor of the shavings with their dung pile after having used shavings for a while. This makes it a lot easier to assign the location of the litter box in the designated barns, or when you are able to provide more space. If you have a stable-setting for your llamas can "go" in their individual stalls. Make sure that you provide them with the shavings that will help them associate their dung from an off-limits area (like the aisle of the stable/barn) so that when you have finished building the walled are, you can easily transition them to the specific area of the barn. Expect some accidents to happen, but you can be confident that if you set it up properly, your llamas will be quick to cooperate.

Labor Saver

The boxes of the males need to be cleaned at least once a week. When the weather is nice, the boxes of the females must be cleaned at least once or twice a week. In hot or rainy weather, the barn should be cleaned more often.

Chapter Eight: Barn Maintenance and Litter Boxes

You will soon realize the time saving convenience of setting an area for your herd of llamas to go to when they need to. Whether you have a smaller herd of about 10 to 12 llamas or a massive number of them, providing these litter boxes for them not only keeps their barn area and living quarters smelling less foul, it also helps you with the cleaning maintenance in the long run. It will shave off valuable labor time.

For bigger herds of up to a hundred llamas, use a small bucket scooper. You can the dump the bucket into a manure spreader. Once you have the stalls stripped you can then sprinkle it with stall freshener and then replace the area with a fresh bed of pine shavings or sawdust. With effective training and practice, you can have a full barn cleaned in two hours.

Make sure you are able to inspect the quality of pine shavings you get from your supplier. Powdery dust will quickly turn to a paste, sticking to the fleece and the skin of the llama. Pine curls will catch in their coats. Wood chips offer very little absorbency.

Chapter Eight: Barn Maintenance and Litter Boxes

You may later experiment and find a better material for the litter box but for starters, stick with fresh sawdust. You can coordinate to get fresh pine sawdust from a nearby mill about two times in a year. Look for consistency that is coarse and scented. Dried shavings are used in a pinch and are stowed away in storage during the winter months.

Once you have set everything in place, maintenance will be so much easier for you. And your llamas will live in better conditions, as a result. There will be fewer flies; you will be able to keep a cleaner barn, giving you more quality, bonding time with your llamas. The only downside to having a low, walled off area is if you intend to show your llamas - they might think the ring to be a massive toile but does make for a cleaner barn.

Extra Care Saves You Plenty

Llamas are hardy animals and need a certain sort of care to thrive well. They will require routine checkups from a certified vet to check them for parasites. Since llamas have a tendency to acquire certain types of parasites, they will

Chapter Eight: Barn Maintenance and Litter Boxes

have to be checked on a monthly basis to monitor their good health, whilst helping to maintain it that way. Aside from the regular wellness visits, another thing to consider putting away money for would be unforeseen events. There are sorts of injuries which need immediate, sometimes, emergency care, like a broken leg which can be life-threatening to llamas. Your commitment to its care would include its expenses for its medical care and the time you will need to provide your llamas needs.

Chapter Nine: Reasons You Should Add Llamas to Your Livestock Herd

There are countless reasons why homesteaders and livestock keepers should consider adding llamas to their farm family. These graceful beasts have a multitude of benefits to those who wish to seek cultivating a life of self-sustainability. For starters, one llama alone is able to provide a pretty substantial quantity of wool. The fleece of the llama can be spun into wool which can later be used to weave mats, rugs, quality of wool produced by llamas depend on

Chapter Nine: Reasons You Should Add Llamas to Your Livestock Herd

the environment they live in, their health as well as their individual colors and patterns.

Benefits of Keeping a Llama

The fleece of the llama provides excellent insulation for the cold weather and your creations is only limited by your imagination. Not only can llamas be easily bred, if this is your desire. There are also individuals who breed llamas for the milk they produce, and others for the meat.

If you are a hiker, a forager of natural, organic plants from the wilderness, a camper or a lover of nature in general, the llama can actually be a great companion on the trails you are familiar and not so familiar with. They are hardy, strong beasts who can carry great loads, saving your back from the cumbersome load that would otherwise tire and slow you down. They are also formidable animals who can be on the lookout and act as centurion to the livestock as well as give warming to the human farm dwellers. Llamas are even trainable to cart and are excellent carters.

Chapter Nine: Reasons You Should Add Llamas to Your Livestock Herd

For their size, llamas are relatively easy to care for, notwithstanding their massive size and mature weight. You don't need a vast expanse of land to keep a couple of llamas comfortably. People with a little bit of land and who have been working on it has been able to successfully integrate a few llamas with other animals they already have. You can use a gelded male (a castrated male llama) to watch over and hold down fort for the other livestock you care for. They can give warning and sound the alert when potential danger looms. Gelded males are also preferred by homesteader to provide them with fleece. The reason for this is that gelded males are more compliant as compared to intact males and/or females.

Llamas for Protection

Livestock such as horses, sheep, goats, or cows, can become quite vulnerable. A pack of wolves will be able to do a lot of damage in the blink of an eye. Llamas are great sentinels to livestock, farm animals and they require less care and training than dogs. They aren't known to be fence

Chapter Nine: Reasons You Should Add Llamas to Your Livestock Herd

jumpers, nor do they just wander off. To top it all off, a lone llama will be able to watch over a great number of animals.

Integrating a llama or two (this is preferred to keeping just one) can be a breeze if you know what to do. With a little guidance from other successful and experienced llama owners, a little research on your part like you are doing now, mingling them into the mix of your other animals won't be difficult at all.

Before introducing new animals to each other, always make sure they have been isolated long enough to ensure they are healthy.

Place the new llama you want to introduce to the mix in another enclosure close by with the other animals in your care. Once you notice that they are all used to each other, remove the barrier separating them and allow them to mingle.

Chapter Nine: Reasons You Should Add Llamas to Your Livestock Herd

Llama Care

Feeding these animals is affordable, inexpensive and easy. They also require less grain. Should you, or a nearby farm, have enough pasture, it would be an added bonus for the grazing llama. During the colder climates when the weather is harsher and there is no field to graze, use grass as an alternative feed.

Surprisingly, llamas eat very little for their size. As big as they come, they have tiny appetites which make feeding them easy. If you are leaving your llama to graze and browse, make sure that the vegetation of the area is acceptable for the llamas. There are a number of plants that can be poisonous to grazing animals therefore, be on the lookout for these around your land.

A mature llama can fare nutritionally grazing in a small field or on a flake or two of hay each day. Border off several small patches of grass and circulate the animals so that each area can recover. To determine the size of each grazing lot, you will have to take stock of how many of them graze.

Chapter Nine: Reasons You Should Add Llamas to Your Livestock Herd

Generally, llamas are robust and very hardy. They do not tend to get sick easily. They are hardier than most but they will require, scheduled routine care so as to enjoy a long healthy life. Groom your llamas regularly and you may get a better collection of fleece when they are scheduled to be sheared.

Make sure that you keep your llamas healthy and free from discomfort and pain. Their toenails can get overgrown especially if they graze in pasture more. Overgrown toenails can affect the mobility of the llama. Toenails are to be cut regularly.

Your llamas should regularly get vaccinated to guard against tetanus. They must also get proper doses of vitamin C and D to lessen the tendency of them developing enterotoxaemia. Keep your llamas in good health by vaccinating them regularly.

Chapter Nine: Reasons You Should Add Llamas to Your Livestock Herd

Housing for Llamas

A barn is not necessary; llamas fairly comfortable in all kinds of weather. Originating from regions where the climate can be harsh at times, doing well in some of the coldest of climates. Their thick wool not only provides them insulation from the cold it also protects them from the heat and rays of the sun as well. However, depending on where you live you will want to provide adequate shelter that would protect them from the elements. A run-in sort of shed that allows them to get in and out of a heavy downpour will be sufficient. A stall setting or a three sided structure will be adequate housing for your llamas. The walls will provide the multitude, some form of safety.

Guarding Against Human Predators

When we consider the possible natural predators of the animals we own, we usually immediately think of and protect our animals from wildlife occurring in the area. Here's good news; a llama gives ample protection from strangers, too.

Chapter Nine: Reasons You Should Add Llamas to Your Livestock Herd

Once they get to know their people they present themselves as brave guards against those who have no business being on the property. A llama discourages any intruder without inflicting injury to the intruder. Dogs make great security guardians for properties. the problem is when an injury to a person is inflicted. Whether it is right or not, the owner of the canine could have to account for personal damages the dog causes. Llamas do the same job of securing perimeter safety without actually hurting an intruder. Their formidable size and their spitting traits can be quite surprising to an intruder but still a pretty harmless manner of chasing off an undesirable.

Other Benefits

The fiber of llamas is thought to be a luxury fiber, in the likes of expensive cashmere and pricey angora. Fleece shows are often held alongside llama shows the fleeces of the llamas are judged against a wide range of criteria. Criteria vary depending on the type of species and breed of the fleece. In a judging competition, some of the most

Chapter Nine: Reasons You Should Add Llamas to Your Livestock Herd

important criteria include density of the fleece, its luster, the fineness, the uniformity and the cleanliness of the wool. Make it a point to bathe and groom your llamas regularly and you too can benefit with the promise of a passive income.

So as to keep your llamas fleece supple and soft, trim them annually. What you collect from the clipping will have many excellent uses. Your imagination will be challenged to think outside the box. Their wool can even be sold or traded to other homesteaders for what you may need for yourself. You can use their fleece or spun wool to barter for goods, for services, or sell it for money.

Keep in mind that llamas are herd animals and will need the company of at least one other llama. The company of another animal, equally docile and even tempered can also be a good choice of pairing to become well adjusted. Make sure that you get a couple of them at least, should you want to employ them as guardians of the livestock and stead.

Chapter Nine: Reasons You Should Add Llamas to Your Livestock Herd

Chapter 10: Summary and Care Sheet

This chapter summarizes all the important things to remember when keeping llamas as pets or as a breeding stock for various uses. Do keep in mind that llamas are one of the most unconventional animals to keep as pets, they may look gentle and easy to maintain but nothing could be further from the truth because as you've read in the previous chapters, you as a keeper have many responsibilities and your time, attention, and commitment is required because this kind of animal isn't just something you can let go off if you realize that you can't take care of it or keep it anymore.

Chapter Ten: Summary and Care Sheet

Let's be proactive when it comes to taking care of these kinds of pets and make sure to follow proper husbandry practices to keep your llamas healthy and happy.

Breeding & Reproduction

- Female llamas are good mothers, and delightful with their babies, horsing around and romping as llamas would.

- Although female llamas have been observed and known to conceive young. The definitely must not be purposefully bred until they are at least 18 to 24 months old.

- Depending on the llama's size and its development, female llamas should only be bred between 18-24 months of age.

Chapter Ten: Summary and Care Sheet

- On the other hand, even though males can technically breed at seven to nine months, they still aren't fully dependable to be proper breeders until they reach three years of age. Wait until the male llamas older before breeding them

- Llamas breed with the male llama on top. The Length of time for copulation may take up to 45 minutes. The act of copulation brings about ovulation roughly around 24 to 36 hours post mating.

- The average gestation period of a llama is about 350 days and a single crias is produced at the end of this period. Twinning doesn't happen very often, in fact, it is quite rare. This hardly ever occurs and typically has a low success rate. A newborn llama, also known as a crias, typically weighs in between 25 to 30 lbs. but can range anywhere from 18 to 40 lbs.

Chapter Ten: Summary and Care Sheet

- Since these amiable animals are induced ovulators, female llamas are able to give birth throughout the year.

- If you should plan on breeding them consider the time, specifically the climate when the female will give birth. You want to avoid birthing in the extreme weather conditions.

- Llama Births normally occur, conveniently during the daytime.

- It takes anywhere from 10-45 minutes from the time both feet and head show up to the time of actual birth

- Unlike most mammals, mother-llamas do not consume the afterbirth, nor do they lick the crias. The young Llama is, called a crias in its native South America.

Chapter Ten: Summary and Care Sheet

- The young llama will start taking steps shortly after birth - typically within an hour.

- The crias should also start nursing within one to two hours upon its emergence.

- The placenta of the mother follows about 4 hours after giving birth. Female llamas are usually bred back three to four weeks after the female llama has given birth. after breeding,

- Pregnancy is determined 21 days after (or more). Lab test examines for progesterone present in the system from a small blood sample extracted from the female llama. Another sign of pregnancy is the female refusal to breed with the same male llama it had previously bred with.

Chapter Ten: Summary and Care Sheet

Care & Feeding

- Those are familiar with and used to the care of other domestic livestock animals, you will learn that llamas are easy to care for. They require minimum veterinary assistance but they will require routine health checkups as well as scheduled vaccinations and deworming.

- When integrating and introducing a new animal to the mix, whether sure or otherwise of the health of the new animal, you will want to isolate it in a pen, within sight of, but separate from the rest, at the onset for about 2 weeks. This two-week period of separation prevents any unintentional introduction of any illnesses. Use this two weeks well and visit with your new llama. These visits will give you both a chance to get acquainted.

- Your watchful observation is critical for both mother and crias. You will need to make sure that the crias is

Chapter Ten: Summary and Care Sheet

eating. The newborn llama should also be eliminating pelleted feces.

- You should have ideally been able to find a vet who is updated and knowledgeable of llama medicine and health care. If he or she is a vet in the area who is inexperienced with llamas, there is information to be had online and from your local city administrators.

- It is strongly advised that any new llama owner have their new llamas be checked out and given a clean bill of health by a veterinarian. The vet should conduct a thorough physical and obtain a stool sample in order to determine if deworming is necessary.

- Although llamas are naturally arid land dwellers, they are able to thrive well in a range of climates, but are often found in colder regions of the Americas.

- Llamas are not only easy to integrate to you collection of livestock and farm animals, they also don't require too much food. Being grazers and browsers of shrubs and trees, nature provides them with the sustenance they need.

- Due to the efficient digestive systems of the llama, they require very little protein. Llama diet can be sustained with hay or by grazing. Again, make sure that you pre-inspect the plants, bushes and trees the llamas may graze on before you actually let them do so. There are too many plants that pose toxic danger to these animals.

- If you plan on grazing your llamas, work it out so that there are only a few animals to a pasture. This is a sustainable method of feeding your grazing animals while allowing grazing plots to regrow.

- Grain is best for working animals. It also works wonders for nursing females, especially when the quality of hay is prime.

Chapter Ten: Summary and Care Sheet

- Salt blocks, which contain selenium, should be available readily at any given time. Granulated minerals are easier to eat because llamas can't lick.

- Avoid over feeding llamas. Grain mixes high in protein and intended to feed other livestock should be avoided by a sturdy llama on a good diet - unless the llama is a nursing female or one that is about to give birth. Llamas have the tendency for bloat if they are overfed or fed with grain.

- Llamas may naturally require less water than most of your other domestic, farm and livestock animals but they should still it at all times. Llamas don't as much during the colder climates and even less when they graze on lush green pasture. They do drink more when it is hot or labored or when it is producing milk.

- If your llamas are pastured on hard or rocky ground, then their toenails will only need to be filed down on occasion. If the graze on pasture then you may have to trim or clip its toenails more frequently. This

Chapter Ten: Summary and Care Sheet

grooming procedure is not difficult to carry out with trimmers used on sheep. However it is strongly advised that you first observe the process of trimming and clipping its toenails as done by an expert, before you do it on your own.

- Llamas are amazingly hardy and robust animals. They have very few problems with disease. However, to ensure that your llamas are in good health, you will need to set up a regular clean up of their litter boxes and have a preventative medicine program.

- The llamas under your care have to be treated for worms every six months. Make it a point to monitor the soil to maintain the integrity of the food your llamas feed on naturally.

Housing & Fencing

- You will have to make a few adjustments before you bring your new llama member home.

Chapter Ten: Summary and Care Sheet

- The barricading fences you put up should be at least four feet high and dog-proofed, if possible. Fencing materials you can utilize can be wooden rails or poles, woven wire, chain link fence, electric barrier, or cattle wire panels. DO not use barbed wire because of the possible injuries it could cause.

- A 3 sided shelter will give sufficient protection to your llamas. If the region you live in experiences severe winters, it will be necessary to have an enclosed shed to house your llamas.

- Heat stress is an important concern if you live in a region that experiences hot or humid weather. A sprinkler will be helpful in this case, giving you llamas provisions to help cool down and maintain a cool body temperature during hot months.

- Outfit a small catch pen to make catching less stressful for you and the animal.

Chapter Ten: Summary and Care Sheet

- Feeding and watering troughs must always be kept clean. These have to high enough to avoid possible contamination of feces. Feeding troughs should also be spacious enough to allow all of the animals to have access.

- Fresh, clean water is essential for your animals. This is especially so during hot months and if you live in a drier and hotter region.

- Shearing of long coated llamas is needed and is highly recommended especially in areas where very hot and humid climates are experienced.

Llama Transport

- Llamas, in their massive size, are surprisingly easy to transport. They do not require any specialized equipment when moving them from one location to another. A covered windproof pickup, van, or utility

Chapter Ten: Summary and Care Sheet

trailer with enough space for the animal to stand comfortably will do the job well.

- Proper ventilation is important in both summer and winter. You can use straw, which makes for excellent bedding material in a contained windproof enclosure. Make sure that you set out hay for food and offer water at free choice to llamas you are transporting every six hours, more frequently if it is warmer, this will all depend on heat. Do not leave the water at the trailer or back of the truck as this will spill if left with them.

- Llamas would typically lie down once they feel the vehicle start to move. If you are transporting crias and mothers on long haul trips, you will have to be mindful about periodically stopping to allow them to nurse and be nursed.

- Should the new llama you are acquiring is coming from out-of-state, make sure to check at least four weeks in advance with your local officials to

Chapter Ten: Summary and Care Sheet

determine if the state you live in requires a veterinarian-issued health certificate.

- You may need a permit number and/or proof of tests carried out for brucellosis, tuberculosis, and other diseases. There are some states which may require permanent identification markings on the animals

Photo Credits

Page 1 Photo by user soapbeard via Flickr.com, https://www.flickr.com/photos/soapbeard/2875945225/

Page 4 Photo by user JuliaBarn via Flickr.com, https://www.flickr.com/photos/alhadley/657575700/

Page 12 Photo by user C Watts via Flickr.com, https://www.flickr.com/photos/watts_photos/32806335175/

Page 19 Photo by user Marie Hale via Flickr.com, https://www.flickr.com/photos/15016964@N02/5912762281/

Page 27 Photo by user Stuart Chalmers via Flickr.com, https://www.flickr.com/photos/gertcha/797757317/

Page 34 Photo by user VanessaC (EY) via Flickr.com, https://www.flickr.com/photos/vanchett/394164618/

Page 42 Photo by user Ronnie Macdonald via Flickr.com, https://www.flickr.com/photos/ronmacphotos/11065786096/

Page 58 Photo by user Karen via Flickr.com, https://www.flickr.com/photos/26686573@N00/14095877806/

Page 69 Photo by user Ronald Woan via Flickr.com,

https://www.flickr.com/photos/rwoan/35204786691/

Page 77 Photo by user Natalia Daporta via Flickr.com,

https://www.flickr.com/photos/ndaporta/9516809194/

Page 87 Photo by user Derek Kaczmarczyk via Flickr.com,

https://www.flickr.com/photos/derek-and-edith/60076227/

References

5 Important Reasons You Should Add Llamas to Your Livestock Herd – Off The Grid News

http://www.offthegridnews.com/how-to-2/5-important-reasons-you-should-add-llamas-to-your-livestock-herd/

All About Raising Llamas - MotherEarthNews.com

https://www.motherearthnews.com/homesteading-and-livestock/all-about-raising-llamas

Alpacas and Llamas: What They Are & Why You Should Keep Them - HobbyFarms.com

https://www.hobbyfarms.com/alpacas-llamas-what-they-are-and-why-you-should-keep-them/**Diseases of Llamas and Alpacas** - Merckvetmanual.com

https://www.merckvetmanual.com/exotic-and-laboratory-animals/llamas-and-alpacas/diseases-of-llamas-and-alpacas

For the Critters - Nose-N-Toes.com

www.nose-n-toes.com/smlc.htm

From The Farm: How About A Pet Llama? - PetAssure.com

https://www.petassure.com/new-newsletters/pet-llamas

What You Need to Know About Owning a Llama –
GalaOnline.org

http://www.galaonline.org/PDF/mentoring_8_659342863.pdf

www.ingramcontent.com/pod-product-compliance
Lightning Source LLC
Chambersburg PA
CBHW070540080426
42453CB00029B/791